Let's Go!

Put each sticker to complete the scene.

T0266483

1

Around Town

Follow the path from ➡ to ➡ while putting each sticker on its matching square. Then, put extra stickers wherever you'd like.

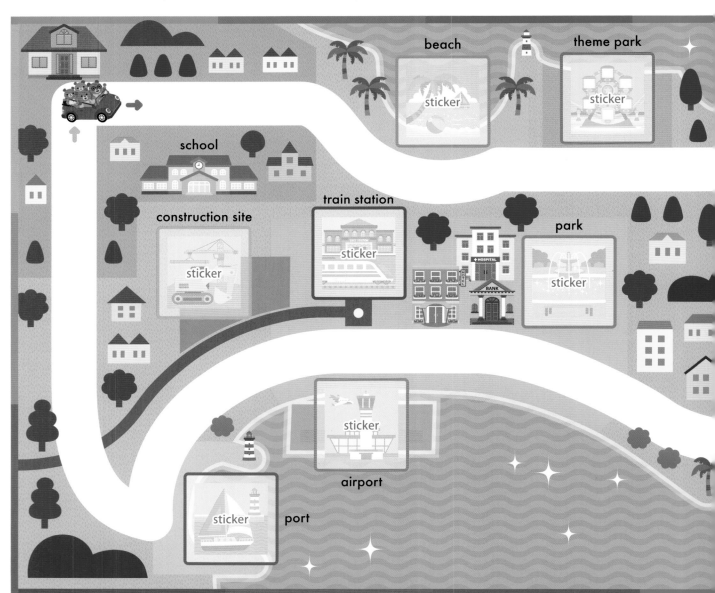

beach

theme park

school

train station

park

construction site

airport

port

example

Good job! Sticker

safari park

aquarium

museum

botanical garden

farm

space museum

ranch

3

Fun in the Sun

Put stickers wherever you'd like to complete the scene at the beach.

example

Sticker
Good job!

LIFE GUARD

LIFE GUARD

5

Theme Park

Put each friend sticker on its matching square. Then, put balloon stickers wherever you'd like.

6

example

Good job!
Sticker

7

Safari Park

Follow the path from ➡ to ➡ while putting the stickers on their matching numbers. Then, put the animal stickers wherever you'd like.

rhinoceros

2 sticker

gorilla

sticker

flamingo

8

giraffe
elephant
zebra
lion
alligator

example

Sticker
Good job!

bison

5 sticker

3 sticker

hippopotamus

tiger

4 sticker

kangaroo

Aquarium

Put the stickers on their matching letters. Then, put the sea creature stickers wherever you'd like.

example

Sticker

Good job!

E sticker

D sticker

Visiting the Museum

Put the ○□☆△♡ stickers on their matching shapes to complete the scene.

Sticker
Good job!

sticker

sticker

pteranodon

mammoth

sticker

plesiosaur

sticker

sticker

triceratops

spinosaurus

Dinosaur Exhibit

Put each bone sticker to complete the dinosaur skeleton.

example

Sticker

Good job!

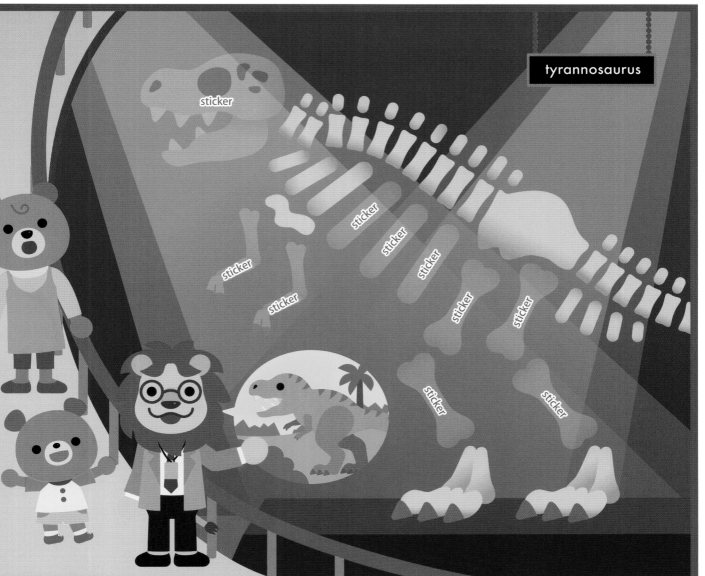

tyrannosaurus

13

Space Museum

Put each sticker on its matching planet. Then, put star stickers wherever you'd like.

Good job!

14

Under the Stars

Put stickers wherever you'd like to
complete the space display.

example

Sticker

Good job!

earth

moon

On the Ranch

Put each baby animal sticker next to its parent.

Sticker
Good job!

horse

sheep

hen

pig

16

Cow Pattern

Add stickers to the cow to create its spot pattern.

example

Sticker

Good job!

COW

17

Farm Fun

Put each sticker on its matching vegetable.

example

Sticker
Good job!

potato

pumpkin

eggplant

onion

carrot

tomato

Botanical Garden

Carefully look at the color of each flower. Then, put the flower stickers with their matching color group.

example

Sticker
Good job!

Neighborhood Park

Follow the path from ➡ to ➡. Then, put stickers wherever you'd like.

example

Sticker
Good job!

ICE CREAM

Train Station

Put friend stickers on the windows of the train. Then, put train stickers on the tracks to complete the scene at the train station.

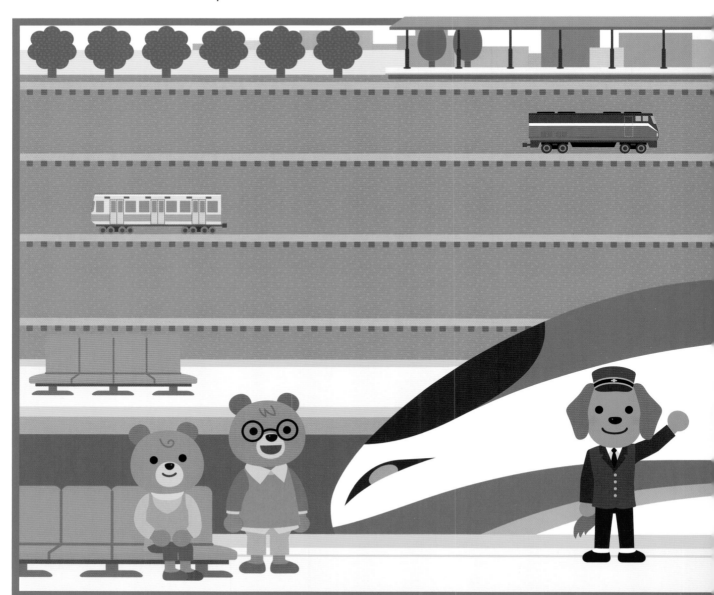

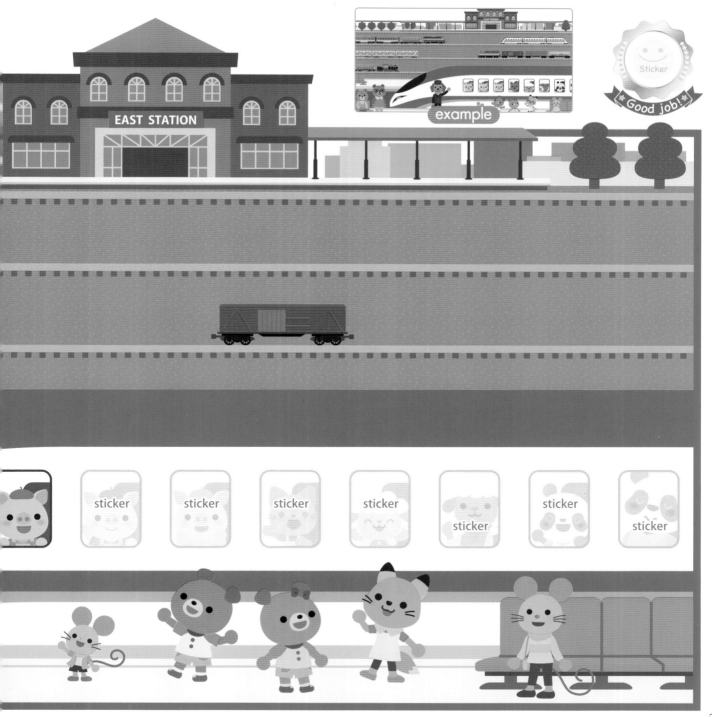

EAST STATION

example

Sticker
Good job!

sticker
sticker
sticker
sticker
sticker
sticker
sticker

23

At the Airport

Put airplane stickers in the sky to complete the scene at the airport.

example

Sticker

Good job!

Maze Picture Puzzle

In the Air

Follow the path from ➡ to ➡ while putting each sticker next to its matching object to complete the picture.

Good job! Sticker

25

At the Port

Put boat stickers wherever you'd like to complete the scene at the port.

example

Sticker

Good job!

marine liner

Construction Site

Put vehicle stickers wherever you'd like to complete the construction site.

example

Sticker

Good job!

cement mixer truck

27

Very Important Workers

What kind of jobs do these people have? Put each sticker on its matching worker.

Sticker
Good job!

police officer

firefighter

flight attendant

construction worker

tour guide

doctor

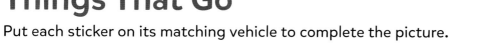

Things That Go

Put each sticker on its matching vehicle to complete the picture.

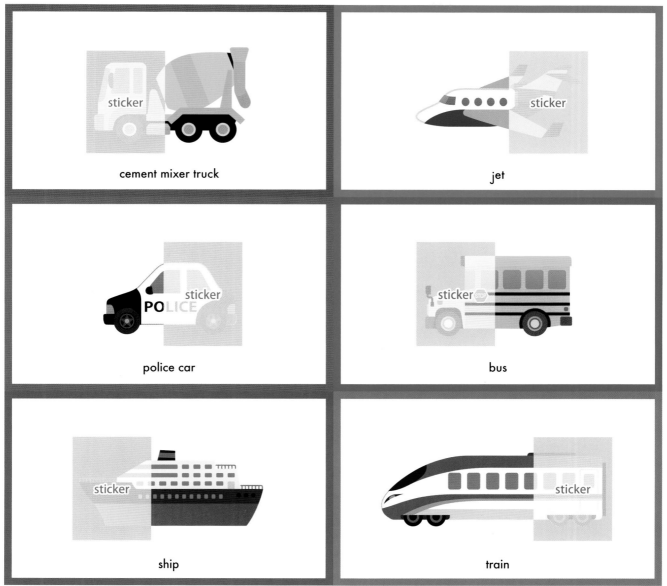

cement mixer truck

jet

police car

bus

ship

train

29

Busy Downtown

Carefully look at the shapes in the picture. Then, put each shape sticker to complete the scene.

shapes

circle | square | triangle | semicircle | rectangle | diamond | heart | star | pentagon | trapezoid

Sticker
Good job!

FIRE STATION
sticker

POST OFFICE
sticker

+ HOSPITAL
sticker

LIFE GUARD

RESTAURANT
sticker

BAKERY

CANDY

sticker

BOOKSTORE

CANDY

31

Flower Shop

Place the bear sticker. Then, add flower stickers to complete each bunch.

FLOWER SHOP

gerbera
sunflower
rose
tulip
carnation
marigold

Fast Food Restaurant

Place the bear sticker. Then, put each food sticker so the tray matches the kids' meal.

Sticker
★ Good job! ★

FAST FOOD

french fries
hot dog
pizza
french fries

👍 KIDS' MEAL

french fries   nuggets

P

hamburger   soda

sticker
P
sticker
sticker
sticker

33

Green Grocer

Place the rabbit sticker. Then, add each vegetable sticker to its matching group.

Good job!

VEGETABLE MARKET

lettuce

corn

broccoli

carrot

tomato

pumpkin

onion

potato

Fruit Stand

Place the koala sticker. Then, look at the color of each fruit sticker and add it to its matching color group.

Good job!

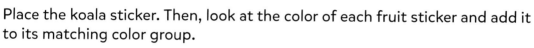

FRUIT STAND

green apple | pear | green grapes | mango

lemon | grapefruit | kiwi | pomegranate

Purple
- grape
- plum — sticker
- blueberry — sticker

Yellow
- banana — sticker
- orange — sticker
- pineapple

Red
- apple
- strawberry — sticker
- cherry — sticker

Green
- avocado — sticker
- lime — sticker
- watermelon

sticker

35

Seafood Market

Place the cat sticker. Then, add each seafood sticker to its matching group.

Sticker

Good job!

SEAFOOD

sticker

salmon

tuna

sticker

tilapia

sticker

lobster

sticker

crab

sticker

shrimp

sticker

scallops

sticker

mussels

sticker

Butcher

Place the dog sticker. There are big portions and small portions at the meat market. Add each sticker to the meat that's the same size.

Good job!

37

Bakery

Place the sheep sticker. Then, add each pastry sticker to its matching group.

Pastry Shop

Place the mouse and pie stickers. Then, decorate the cake with your favorite stickers.

example

Sticker
★ Good job! ★

PASTRY SHOP

sticker

sticker

sticker

Classification
Candy Shop

Place the leopard sticker. Then, add each candy sticker to its matching group.

Ice Cream Shop

Place the pig sticker. Then, carefully look at the number of scoops on each cone and put the ice cream sticker with the same number of scoops.

Good job!

41

At the Pharmacy

Place the elephant sticker. Then, add each sticker to its matching group.

At the Bookstore

Place the squirrel sticker. Then, look at the size of the books and put each book sticker on the same size shadow.

 example

 Sticker · Good job!

At the Toy Shop

Place the bear sticker. Then, add each toy sticker to its matching toy.

Good job!

At the Clothing Store

Place the bear sticker. Then, add stickers to decorate the dress.

example

Sticker
Good job!

At the Restaurant

Put drink stickers on the table so everyone has a drink. Then, place the the food stickers on the table so everyone has something to eat.

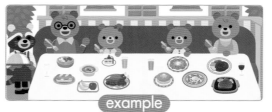

example

Sticker

Good job!

47

We're Home!

Put "Good," "Wonderful," and "Like" stickers on your favorite
things. Then, use your leftover stickers, if any, wherever you'd like!

example

Sticker

Good job!

We're home!

MONSTERS

PETER PAN

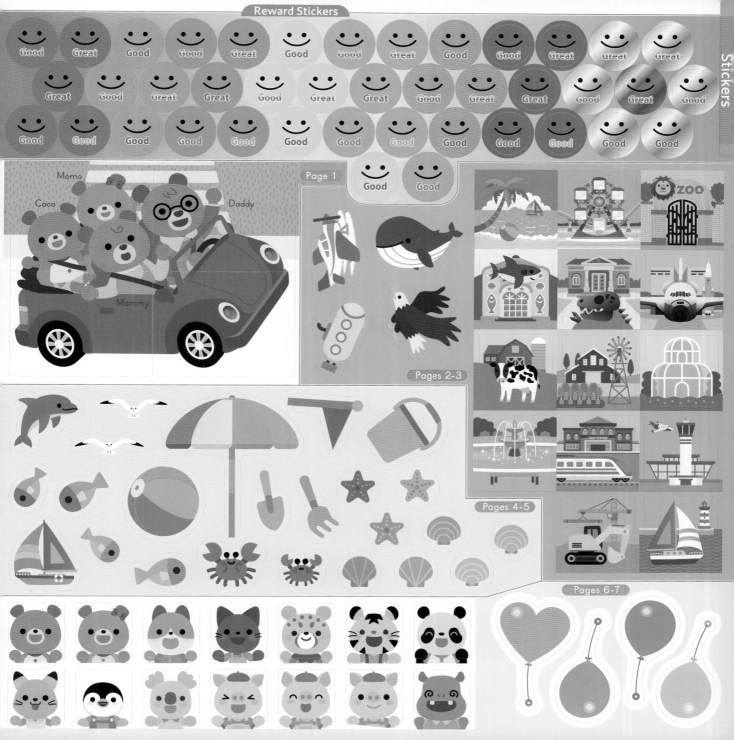

Reward Stickers

Stickers

Good Great Good Good Great Good Good Great Good Good Great Great Great
Great Good Great Great Good Good Great Good Great Great Good Great Good
Good Good Good Good Good Good Good Good Good Good Good Good Good Good

Good Good

Page 1

Momo
Coco
Daddy
Mammy

Pages 2-3

ZOO

Pages 4-5

Pages 6-7

Pages 10-11

Pages 8-9

Pages 12-13

Page 14

Page 16

Page 15

Page 17

Page 18

Page 19

Pages 20-21

Stickers

Pages 22 -23

Page 25

Page 24

Page 26

oil tanker

container ship

Page 27

yacht

sailboat

xcavator

bulldozer

truck

fishing boat

Page 28

boat

POLICE

HOTEL

MAIL

Stickers

TABLE MARKET

Pages 30-31

POLICE

STOP

TION

KIDS

HOSPITAL

Page 29

Page 32

Page 33

Page 35

Page 34

Page 36

Page 37

Page 38

Page 39

Page 40

Page 41

Page 42

HAND SOAP

TOOTHPASTE FOR KIDS

919

MONSTERS

FLOWERS

SPACE

Colors

PIANO

PINOCCHIO

The Little Mermaid

PETER PAN

The Frog Prince

Cinderella

Page 43

Page 44

Page 45

Pages 46-47

Page 48